AMERICA'S

Published by Gallery Books
A Division of W H Smith Publishers Inc.
112 Madison Avenue
New York, New York 10016

Produced by
Brompton Books Corp.
15 Sherwood Place
Greenwich, CT 06830

ISBN 0-8317-0354-7

Printed in Hong Kong

10 9 8 7 6 5 4 3 2

COUNTRYSIDE

TEXT   ROBIN LANGLEY SOMMER

DESIGN   MIKE ROSE

GALLERY BOOKS
An imprint of W.H. Smith Publishers Inc.
112 Madison Avenue
New York, New York 10016

Photo Credits

Ulrich Ackermann: 47, 76, 109, 130, 158-59, 210.
Tom Algire Photography: 18, 26, 32, 35, 41,
    44-45, 63, 68, 69, 107, 122-23, 126-27, 140-41,
    220-21, 226-27.
Arkansas Department of Parks and Tourism: 191.
Bear Photo/Joe Carini: 188 bottom, 195.
Chris Beck: 96 top.
Marcello Bertinetti and Angela White Bertinetti: 1,
    39, 56, 58, 59, 60, 61, 65, 71, 82-83, 101 top,
    105, 108, 129, 148 top, 186, 187, 189 top,
    192-93, 194, 208 bottom, 209 bottom, 214-15.
Jeff Blechman: 104.
Camera Hawaii, Inc./ Werner Stoy: 79.
Comstock: 208 top.
Cyr Color Photo Agency: Joe Craighead (19),
    William Gates (155), Perry Ladd (97 top), Charles
    McNulty (48 top), Otto Pfeifer (48 bottom), Joseph
    Quinn (225 top), Bruce Romick (30 bottom, 173),
    Randolph Small (115), Harry Williams (114).
Carlo and Valeria De Fabianis: 85.
FPG International: N Groffman (42-43), J Hailey
    (57), J Blank (66-67), D Hallinan (92-93), C H
    Smith (152-53), F Dole (206-07), J F Buchholz
    (226).
Jeff Gnass: 3-6, 15, 20-21, 22-23, 24-25, 27, 40,
    46, 50-51, 55, 62, 78, 88-89, 91, 98-99, 106, 111,
    116-17, 140, 144, 148 bottom, 150-51, 205, 209
    top, 219, 232, 240.
Stewart M Green: 33, 149.
H Armstrong Roberts: 31, 95, 125, 131, 136-37,
    189 bottom, P Avis (30 top), D Winston (64), J
    Gleiter (72-73, 84), Joura (94), A Griffin (112-13),
    Ed Cooper (120-21), W McKinney (124), R Lamb
    (156-57), M Thonig (222-23), F Sieb (229), R
    Krubner (233).

Louisiana Office of Tourism: 225 bottom.
Rick McIntyre: 139 both, 142-43, 228.
M A C Miles: 49.
Jack Olson: 145, 154, 172.
Douglas K Paulding: 146-47.
Ron Ruhoff: 102-03.
Irene Hinke Sacilotto: 74-75.
Allan Seiden: 77, 80-81, 87, 101 bottom,
    188 top, 197, 198, 212-13, 216-17.
Jim Shives: 86, 100, 135, 199, 211.
Jerry Sieve: 28-29, 52-53, 118, 119, 128, 132-33,
    138, 161, 162-64, 167, 171, 176-77 178, 179,
    182-83, 196, 201, 202-03, 230-31, 234-35,
    236-37.
The Stockhouse, Inc: K Cole: 38 top, 185.
Tennessee Tourist Development Division: 190.
Mireille Vautier and Aline de Nanxe: 36-37, 38
    bottom, 96 bottom, 165, 166, 168-69, 174-75,
    180-81, 204.
Vermont Travel Division: 16-17
Wyoming Travel Commision: 97 bottom.

Acknowledgments

Special thanks to Barbara Paulding
Thrasher and Gillian Goslinga, who
edited this book, and to Jean
Chiaramonte Martin, who did the
picture research.

3-6   *Autumn touches the Vermont countryside.*

INTRODUCTION

Perhaps no other land has the incredible scenic variety to be found in America's countryside. Many factors have conspired to contribute to this diversity: the enormous size of the North American continent, its geologic and climatic history, and the relentless westward movement of its settlers, which resulted in the acquisition of such far-flung and disparate regions as Alaska, Hawaii and the Southwest.

The country roads of America lead deep into the Florida Everglades, high into the Rocky Mountains—the great stone spine of the continent— and far into the Painted Desert of Arizona. They pass through the picturesque towns of New England, the tree-shaded streets of the Middle West, and the bayous of Louisiana. New vistas open up at every turn. On the East Coast, it might be a glimpse of the Green Mountains of Vermont, or New Hampshire's Franconia Notch. Farther south is the expanse of Chesapeake Bay, Kentucky Bluegrass country, the Great Smoky Mountains, Virginia's rolling hills, and the flatlands of Georgia and northern Florida.

Midwestern country roads offer views of flourishing cornfields, well-kept towns and farms, the great Ohio River wending its way toward the Mississippi, and the wooded hills of what was once called the Northwest Territory. Here the Mound Builders left a record of their high civilization in the form of great earthworks used for ceremonial rites and as burial grounds. And their successors, Eastern Indian tribes who had been pushed steadily westward by European colonists, united to make a heroic but hopeless stand against the invaders.

The red clay roads of the Deep South lead through pine woods somnolent in the heat, small hamlets along the Mississippi, and antebellum plantations built on sugar cane, cotton and tobacco. Their white columns and porticoes are shaded by ancient live oaks draped in Spanish moss and surrounded by white magnolias and multicolored azaleas. Roadside stands sell pecans and fresh produce. Family and community ties are still strong here, and leisurely groups congregate on front porches to review the day's events and the prospects for tomorrow.

In the Southwest, tenacious Indian and Mexican farmers were the first to cultivate a wild and beautiful land whose rich soil required irrigation to make it productive. Even now, great tracts of wilderness remain untamed, marked by soaring arches of red sedimentary rock, wind-sculpted dunes, and jagged mountain peaks. North of here, on the Great Plains, are vast fields of wheat and other grains threaded by ribbons of highway that unroll toward an ever-receding horizon. Towns may be many miles apart, but the people retain the self-reliant spirit of their sod-busting pioneer ancestors and do for themselves and one another in the traditional way.

The Rocky Mountains comprise one of the greatest natural wonders of the continent, extending from northern Alaska to the Southwest and rising in Canada between Alberta and British Columbia. These impassable peaks delayed settlement of the Far West until the nineteenth century, when enterprising miners, roadbuilders and railroad men finally made their way through. Today, country roads in the Rockies wind past sheep and cattle grazing in the foothills and climb past the sites of old mining towns to wilderness areas like Yellowstone National Park, where Wyoming, Montana and Idaho meet. Here on the Continental Divide rise the headstreams of rivers flowing to both the Atlantic and the Pacific—the Missouri and the Snake. Moose, deer, bear and antelope frequent the forests of the northern Rockies. Fields full of wildflowers and clear streams that widen into beaver ponds form part of an ever-changing landscape.

The West Coast enjoys a steady stream of warm winds borne by the Pacific Ocean. Southern California shares the hot climate of the Southwest, while the northern part of the state is more temperate, shading into the Pacific Northwest. The country roads of the West Coast may overlook great stretches of sandy beach, jutting headlands that loom out over the Pacific, or tall stands of timber still untouched by man. The Cascade Mountains, crowned by snow and ice, extend south from British Columbia into northern California, threaded by waterfalls and studded by gem-like lakes. The countless arms of Puget Sound give access to the Inside Passage through the grandeur of coastal Alaska, and the Alaska Highway provides an overland route to the peaks and glaciers of America's last frontier.

The country roads of Hawaii link East and West, old and new, sea and sky. They border the islands' multicolored sand beaches, bisect its many luxuriant plantations, and rise steeply into the volcanic mountains clothed in tropical vegetation. Along the way are traces of Hawaii's colorful past, from the original Polynesian settlers through the missionaries and whalers of the nineteenth century to the Chinese and Japanese who came as field hands and stayed to become businessmen, teachers and politicians.

The diversity of America's towns and people reflects the many ethnic, cultural and geographic strands that have been woven together to form the nation. New England towns, with their white clapboard churches and village greens, are strongly evocative of Old England, whence so many settlers of the eastern seaboard came. Virginia retains echoes of the plantation aristocracy that made it so important in colonial history, while West Virginia partakes more of the hardy pioneers and mountain men who left the coastal regions in favor of greater freedom and autonomy. Florida has traces of its Spanish origins in cities like St Augustine and the beautiful estate called Vizcaya, overlooking Biscayne Bay. And the tourists have not displaced the hard-working farmers, fishermen and businessmen who first developed the resources of the state.

California and the Southwest maintain close ties with their Indian and Hispanic past in the form of historic missions, adobe pueblos, and vast tracts of ranchland dominated by *haciendas* that may date from the days when these lands belonged to Mexico. French Louisiana lives on in the Cajun communities of the bayous, the lacy iron grillework of the Vieux Carre, and New Orleans' annual Mardi Gras celebration.

Homesick New Englanders who settled the Pacific Northwest named the cities of Salem and Portland, Oregon, and built neat, tree-shaded towns that recalled their colonial heritage. The scenic Columbia River Basin is dotted with these towns and farms. Farther north, the Indian leader Seattle was honored for his help to incoming settlers when a tiny village on Puget Sound was named for him.

East of the Rockies, all the way to the original Northwest Territory, Indian place names recall the original inhabitants of the country: Cheyenne, Pawnee, Mandan, Illinois, Iowa, Mississippi and many more. Today, the Great Plains echo to the sound of huge harvesters rather than to herds of buffalo on the move, but it is easy to imagine a warlike band of Plains Indians sweeping across the prairies to defend their hunting grounds.

America's countryside is truly a treasure house of scenic beauties that take on new meaning in the context of the past and the future. As Albert Einstein said so movingly, 'One cannot help but be in awe when he contemplates the mysteries of eternity, of life, of the marvelous structure of reality.'

FARMLANDS

America's farmlands are among the richest and most extensive in the world. It was the lure of this land that drew so many immigrants across the oceans to take their chance in the uncharted wilderness of the North American continent. Their hopes were not disappointed. As they cleared the land of wood and stone and pressed farther west, they continued to find good soil, abundant water, and a climate conducive to agriculture.

The nation's rural heritage remains apparent today, despite the pervasive effects of modern technology. Family farms still flourish side by side with larger tracts run by 'agribusiness' concerns. New England farmers contend with the same stony soil that their ancestors encountered as a legacy of the Ice Age. And a New England spring still signals maple sugar time, when the trees are tapped and the sap brought in, sometimes by a yoke of oxen or a horse still restless from long winter confinement.

Across the country, dairy farms operate wherever there is good pasturage and water. Spotted Holstein, Jersey and Guernsey cows add color to the landscape as they graze in their green fields, keeping a watchful eye on the spring calves that cavort around them with the high spirits of youth. Cattle raising is still a major industry in the West, where wild Mexican longhorns were first herded in Texas. The great trail drives have ended, but the cattle remain and so do the cowboys and their agile horses, who have proved irreplaceable even in an age of mechanization.

'Amber waves of grain' still ripple across the Great Plains, and the Indian corn adopted by the Pilgrims is a staple of the American diet almost 400 years later. Grapevines introduced from Europe have flourished in the soil of New York State, California and Washington. Citrus fruits, apples, melons, fresh vegetables and root crops are harvested in abundance. Cotton still grows in the deep black soil of the Mississippi Delta, and southern tobacco is a major cash crop. Flowering orchards of cherry, almond and pear beautify the countryside, and innumerable nuts and berries that once grew wild are now cultivated for the market.

Despite the fact that machinery has taken over many of the backbreaking chores of earlier days, farming remains a special kind of vocation, attuned to the vicissitudes of wind and weather, sensitive to the stirrings of nature in all its manifestations. American farmers are in touch with their land and strengthened by their daily contact with the things that matter most.

15 Alaska's fertile Matanuska Valley, near Anchorage, was settled by Midwestern farmers who fled the Depression era Dust Bowl.

16/17 A winter farmyard tinged with violet in Montpelier, Vermont.

18 Full corn cribs testify to the abundance of a Midwestern harvest.

19 Haying is still an occasion for both hard work and celebration, in the tradition of rural America.

20/21 A Mission Valley farm near Ronan, Montana, on an August morning.

22/23 A field of taro, source of the Hawaiian food poi, carpets the Hanalei Valley.

24/25   *A prosperous, well-kept ranch in central Oregon's Crook County.*

26   *A striking barn mural recalls the Chippewa heritage of Lincoln County, Wisconsin.*

27 Cotton is a major crop in Oklahoma's Washita region.

28/29 Modern-day cowboys at work on an Arizona ranch.

30 top   A flowering apple tree and sun-gold dandelions herald spring on a New Hampshire farm.

30 bottom   An Amish farmer keeps to the old ways in Lancaster, Pennsylvania.

31   New Englanders tap their trees for maple syrup and sugar in the early spring.

32   *A sleek herd of prime Holstein dairy cows
in rural Wisconsin, heart of the Dairy Belt.*

33 *A rancher checks up on his stock in the shadow of the Sangre de Cristo Mountains.*

COUNTRY ROADS

The pleasure of a ride in the country lies partly in the unexpected: each turn of the road may disclose a view of some natural beauty unlooked for, some quiet haven, some byway leading still farther into the unknown. The American countryside abounds in such delightful surprises.

If one travels the Northeast, a country road may take him to the rocky cliffs of Maine, the Berkshires of western Massachusetts, the sculpted dunes of Cape Cod or Nantucket. Fall foliage here is a glory of crimson, gold and orange that sweeps up the hillsides and turns the valleys into wonderlands. Trim red and white barns and weathered farmhouses alternate with small towns where the general store still serves as the hub of community life. In the coastal towns of Connecticut, Rhode Island and Maine, fishing remains a way of life, and men congregate on the docks to exchange news of the tides and weather forecasts. In eastern Pennsylvania, Amish farmers plow their fields with teams of horses and paint hex signs on their barns to protect their livestock.

Country roads through the South lead to the Great Smoky Mountains of Tennessee and North Carolina, their ridges veiled always in misty haze. Or to the longest cave system in the world, hidden beneath a vast limestone plateau in Kentucky. Other roads travel through the scenic Ozarks and Virginia's beautiful Shenandoah Valley. Still farther south is the vast slow-moving river called the Florida Everglades, with its endless miles of shimmering saw grass punctuated by lofty palms and mangroves.

Midwestern roads may lead through remnants of the great pine forests that once covered this entire section of the country, or along the wide Ohio and Missouri Rivers that empty into the Mississippi. Other routes lead to the Great Lakes and the region's many smaller lakes and waterways, where wooded campsites attract weekenders and vacationers from big-city life in Chicago, Detroit, Cleveland and other urban centers. Still farther west, the huge cornfields of Iowa and the wheatfields of the Great Plains states unroll to the horizon.

The roads of the Southwest wind through cattle country, oil fields, and spectacular wilderness settings like Utah's Bryce Canyon, where pink pinnacles and spires loom over a maze of twisting ravines. In Arizona, the mild-deep Grand Canyon of the Colorado River widens to 10 miles across and discloses some two billion years of the earth's history in its sheer red walls.

On the West Coast, country roads lead from southern California's desolate Death Valley to the Pacific shoreline and a distant view of the Channel Islands, teeming with seabirds and seals. As the sandy beaches of southern California give way to the steep, rocky shoreline of the Pacific Northwest, the redwoods tower above all other trees. The pristine Cascade Mountains march toward Canada, and the wonders of Alaska reveal themselves from Glacier Bay to the golden Kobuk Valley.

35   Peaceful Cades Cove, in Tennessee's Great Smoky Mountains National Park.

36/37   Two hardy bikers make their way into the immensity of Arches National Park, Utah.

38 top   A roadside chile stand strikes a bright note along a Southwestern highway.

38 bottom   A camper trundles into the desert in search of wide skies and solitude.

39   One of California's many faces: a homey general store near the glittering resort of Palm Springs.

40   Scenic Skyline Drive in the Blue Ridge Mountains of Virginia.

41   A legion of giants guards the way through California's Sequoia National Park.

42/43   Stirrings of spring along a winding road in Hollis, New Hampshire.

44/45 Colorado's stony San Juan Mountains loom over a remote valley.

46 The Green Bank Hollow covered bridge takes travelers across a stream in South Danville, Vermont.

47 A steep stretch of the rugged 1500-mile Alaska Highway.

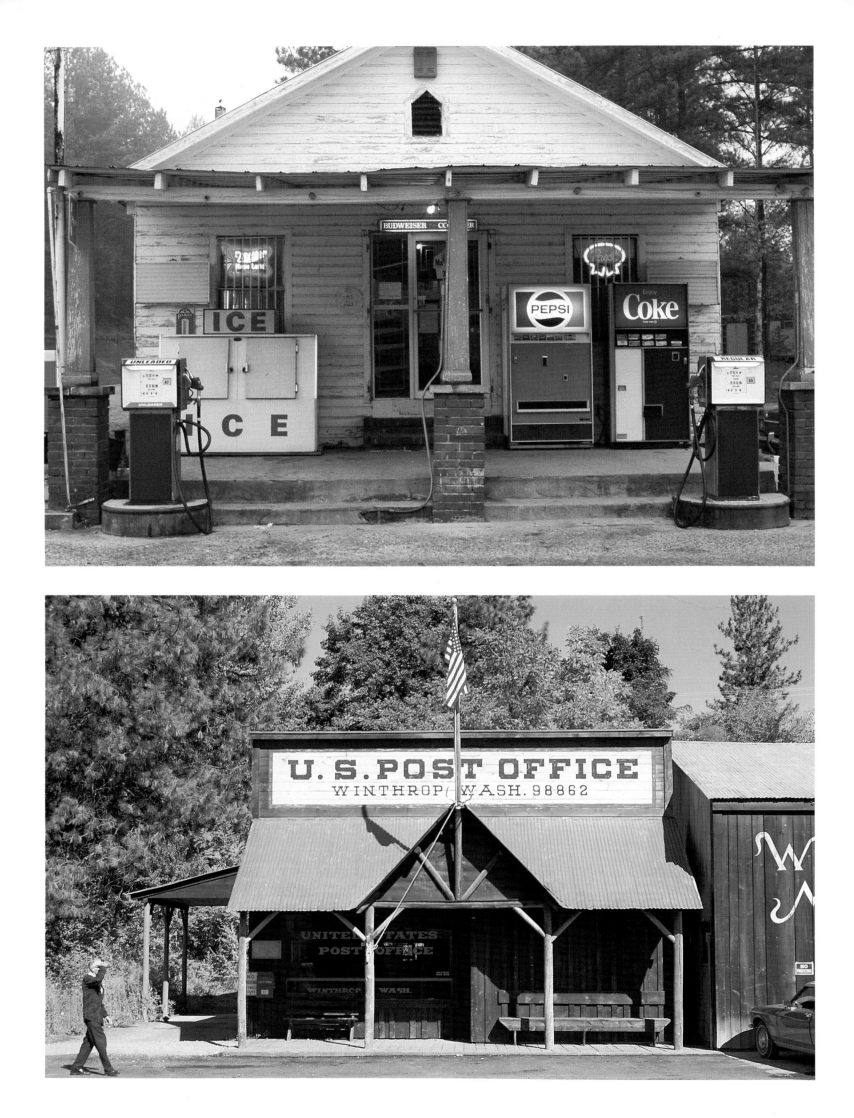

48 top Trading post and gathering place, a country store in Columbia County, Georgia.

48 bottom The frontier-style post office in rural Winthrop, Washington.

49 Signs of the times accumulate on a venerable New England general store.

50/51 Old Kentucky Home: The Stonereath Farm in beautiful Bourbon County.

52/53 Ribbons of light mark the Beeline Highway (US 87) between Phoenix and Payson, Arizona.

THE EAST COAST

The East Coast of America has been shaped by the Atlantic Ocean, not only geographically, but socially as well. Many of the country's first settlements were founded on streams and bays of the Atlantic, and its coastal and inland waterways still serve as arteries of trade and transportation. Fish from its waters provided food and revenue to early colonists, and fleet merchant ships launched from Boston, Providence and Wilmington carried goods around the world.

The Atlantic can appear in many guises, from the stormy gray waves of a New England northeaster to the placid harbors of Charleston and Savannah and the sparkling blue-green waters off the coast of southern Florida. Fierce storms sometimes ravage the Outer Banks of the Carolinas and inundate low-lying coastal communities. A series of 22 lighthouses helps guide vessels along the Intracoastal Waterway, a sheltered water route that makes use of the many rivers, estuaries, sounds, inlets and canals between Boston and Miami.

The land adjoining the shoreline is relatively flat, often sandy or marshy, sometimes wooded and watered by clear streams. Where urban sprawl has not intruded, the wildlife of the salt marshes remains abundant: muskrats, mink, otters, foxes and raccoons. Shore birds forage for mollusks, and the hungry gulls eat almost anything they can find. Graceful grasses, cattails and lilies flourish with the pink hibiscuslike flowers of the marsh mallow.

Farther inland, coniferous and deciduous trees form extensive woodlands laced with brooks and waterfalls. The woods are home to rabbits, opossums, deer and many different kinds of songbird. Less visible, but very much a part of the eastern woodlands, are the colorfully marked box turtle, the striped forest snail, and the nocturnal skunk. Wildcats are increasingly rare in the populous East, but occasionally a cougar is spotted in wilderness areas of Georgia and Florida like the 700-square-mile Okefenokee Swamp.

The Florida peninsula has been a land of legend since Juan Ponce de Leon came looking for the Fountain of Youth in 1513. But the beauties of its wide, tropical beaches, warm climate, profuse flowers and cloudless skies were little known until Florida was linked to the rest of the country by rail in the late nineteenth century. Now the interior is filled with citrus groves and cattle ranches, while the two coasts are among the nation's most popular resort areas. Fortunately, much of this beautiful state remains undeveloped, tempting explorers into the Everglades and along the keys that extend down into the Caribbean almost as far as Cuba.

55 *An old life-saving station adrift in a sea of beach grass on Cape Cod.*

56 Maine lobstermen relax after an arduous day at sea.

57 A cottage garden and colorful buoys share a seaside home in Groton Point, Connecticut.

58 The Gulf of Maine takes fire in the setting sun off Mount Desert Island.

59 A lone seagull surveys the fog-enshrouded coast of northern New England.

60   The beach at St Petersburg, on Florida's Gulf Coast.

61 top   A pelican observes the activity at Flamingo harbor in the Everglades.

61 bottom   The Gulf Coast of Florida is famous for the number and variety of seabirds that flock there.

62   The windmill at Eastham, Massachusetts, oldest of the Cape Cod mills.

63   Cape Henry Lighthouse at Fort Story, Virginia, makes a bold geometric statement against the skyline.

64 *Blueberries ripen in the sandy woods along the New England coast.*

65 *Wheeling home from a day at the beach in York, Maine.*

66/67 A tranquil evening scene along the Atlantic coast.

68 Chincoteague National Wildlife Refuge is a haven for seabirds and marsh dwellers of the Virginia shoreline.

69 Fishing and boating are part of Maryland's way of life, as seen here on Tilghman Island.

THE WEST COAST AND BEYOND

California and the Pacific Northwest share a coast on the world's largest ocean, which helps to create the delightful climate enjoyed by these regions. Warm winds and currents moderate the heat and drop ample rain on the farmlands, forest and cities west of the Cascade Range. California's beaches reveal themselves in their natural beauty by early or evening light, when all traces of human occupation are erased by the surf and the silence is broken only by the rhythmic pounding of the breakers and the random cry of a gull. Tidal pools populated by brightly colored crabs, starfish and sea anemones yield up their secrets to the solitary walker or would-be naturalist.

North of San Diego, Long Beach and Santa Monica is the wild beauty of Big Sur, where cliffs fall away to the sea and rugged rock formations suggest a medieval fortress. South of the Monterey Peninsula is the Point Lobos State Reserve, where more than 250 kinds of wild animals are protected, including the sea otter, which was almost extinct a hundred years ago as a result of the fur trade. Sea lions roar among the rocks, and migrating whales may be spotted far out at sea.

Off the coast of Oregon is the Columbia River Bar, where the West's greatest river empties into the Pacific. Fantastically eroded sea stacks protrude from the coastal waters, and bluff headlands dominate the shoreline. The waters of the Pacific are tamed when they flow into Washington's Puget Sound, a great inland sea that provides access to Canada and Alaska.

No one who has traveled Alaska will ever forget the frigid beauty of Glacier Bay or the immensity of the Tongai National Forest, the largest on the continent. Southwest of Anchorage, the Alaska Peninsula and the Aleutian Islands curve into the North Pacific, separating it from the Bering Sea. The sparsely inhabited islands extend southwest for more than a thousand miles to form what the native Aleuts called 'the land of the smoky sea.'

Another kind of Pacific paradise lies more than 2000 miles southwest of San Francisco: the tropical islands of Hawaii. They are the peaks of a chain of submerged volcanic mountains, two of which, Mauna Loa and Kilauea, are still active. As James Michener wrote in *Hawaii*, 'In violence the island lived, and in violence a great beauty was born.'

The name 'Hawaii' summons up images of the sparkling waters off Diamond Head, a field of orchids heavy with dew, palm trees tracing their graceful lines against the sky, and glistening volcanic sand rimmed with foam. Hawaii is all this and more, a land unique unto itself. Both Hawaii and Alaska form the westernmost extension of America's frontier, where wilderness remains unexplored and where cultural diversity is mainstream.

71   A pristine California beach along the Big Sur Highway.

72/73   Washington's Olympic Peninsula has been carved by wind and tide.

74/75   Six-hundred-pound sunbathers enjoy St Paul's Beach in Alaska's Pribilof Islands.

76 *A three-mile boardwalk creates community in the Panhandle town of Ketchikan, Alaska.*

77 *A bush pilot delivers the mail by seaplane on Alaska's Kodiak Island.*

78 Tiny St Peter's Church at Kahaluu Bay, Hawaii, occupies the former site of a Polynesian temple.

79 A sailboat makes its way into the oncoming night off the island of Hawaii.

80/81 Anxious tourists take a guided tour of the steep ridge above Kalaupapa, Hawaii.

82/83 The landmark Lone Cypress clings to its rocky perch above the Pacific between Carmel and Monterey, California.

84 On Cape Disappointment, Washington, Canby Light warns sailors of the dangerous Columbia River Bar.

85 California's Point Lobos State Reserve is home to seabirds, otters and sea lions.

86 Hawaii's Annual Wahine Fishing Tournament is a popular outdoor festival.

87 Prize-winning halibut advertise fishing charters in the Alaska town of Homer.

88/89 Homer is located on a spit of land that extends into Kachemak Bay from the scenic Kenai Peninsula.

TOWNS

Small-town America has been both idealized and criticized by scores of American writers, most of whom went to the city to make their marks on the literary world. Undoubtedly, there are still many differences between small-town and urban life. But in the electronic age, most American towns are neither as idyllic nor as provincial as they have sometimes been depicted.

Towns have often grown up around an occupation or a way of life that contributes to local solidarity and a strong sense of community. Many towns bordering the two coasts, the Gulf of Mexico, and major inland waterways are dependent upon fishing for their livelihood. The rural Midwest, the Great Plains states, and much of the South and Southwest are preoccupied with farming and ranching. Between Boston and Atlanta, there are scores of 'company towns' that look to a local factory, mill, mine or other business enterprise for their continued prosperity. University towns all over the country take their tone from a major educational institution, and resort towns depend upon seasonal influxes of tourists; their populations shrink dramatically when the swimming, boating or skiing season ends.

The towns of California and the Southwest show their Hispanic and Indian origins in adobe buildings with red-tiled roofs, spacious, tree-shaded plazas, and cool patios hung with flowering vines. Louisiana's French accent is carried out in wrought-iron balconies, strong, bitter coffee, and the Cajun *patois* of the bayou country. New England still has a colonial flavor, with its village greens and wayside inns and taverns.

Strong ethnic communities survive among the American Indians, the Eskimos of Alaska, and newly arrived immigrant groups including the Hispanic and the Vietnamese. The common thread is a pride in ancestry, language, belief, traditional skills and handicrafts—all the things that bond people into social groups and are handed down as values from one generation to the next.

Inevitably, there are clashes between old and new ways of doing things, between the elders and the up-and-coming generation, which tests itself against the wisdom of the group. But on the positive side are important intangibles: a strong support system in time of need, local and civic responsibility, shared goals and enterprises, mutual affirmation. The future of the American town seems safe so long as people maintain strong ties with one another and with the places that nurture them and give meaning to their lives.

91 A spotless New England village church is framed by maples in fall foliage.

92/93 Secluded Waterville, Vermont, has a population of 470.

94   An old pioneer cabin preserves the frontier heritage of Washington state.

95   The Grist Mill at the Wayside Inn in Sudbury, Massachusetts, is a reminder that many old towns were sited on streams and rivers to power grain and saw mills.

96 top   Main Street in Ouray, Colorado, invites one on a walk into the past.

96 bottom   Iron-wheeled wagons provided a bumpy ride through Utah mining towns a century ago.

97 top   The old 89er Mine is now a tourist attraction in Oklahoma City.

97 bottom   Picturesque South Pass City has changed little since Wyoming frontier days.

98/99   The fabulous Corn Palace at Mitchell celebrates one of South Dakota's most important crops.

100   A country church and its outbuildings in far-northern Circle, Alaska.

101 top   The first California settlements grew up around Spanish missions like San Carlos Borromeo at Carmel.

101 bottom   The simplicity of Father Damien's Chapel in Kalawao recalls the faith of the Belgian missionary who spent his live in service to Hawaii's outcast lepers.

102/103   The Colorado town of Blackhawk looks almost like a toy village for a model railroad set.

104　A resident of Martha's Vineyard, Massachusetts, relaxes on the porch of the local post office.

105　Captain Tony's Saloon is a popular watering hole in unhurried Key West, Florida.

106 The Harriet Dean House in Springfield, Illinois, is part of the Lincoln Home National Historic Site.

107 The Joseph Jefferson mansion, Live Oak Gardens, in Louisiana.

108 St Augustine, Florida, is the nation's oldest city, founded by the Spanish in 1565.

109 The Norwegian fishing town of Petersburg, on Kupreanof Island in Alaska's Panhandle region.

LAKES AND RIVERS

One of the New World's most compelling attractions during the age of exploration and settlement was the many streams, lakes and rivers that watered the land. They promised good farming and fishing, and provided routes into the interior of North America. As population increased, they served as arteries of trade, communication and expansion. American history is inseparable from the story of such rivers as the Mississippi, the Missouri, the Columbia, the Rio Grande, to say nothing of the Great Lakes, the Erie Canal, and the Chesapeake and Ohio Canal.

Today, the nation's lakes and rivers are increasingly important recreational and ecological resources. Far-sighted conservationists have established the importance of clean, fresh water to the entire ecosystem. Waterways that had been polluted by commerce and industry are being cleaned up and restocked with fish. Those that remain unspoiled have been protected by law, or reserved as part of our wilderness heritage. All 50 states have some unique or beautiful body of water to show.

In the Pacific Northwest, the Cascade Range is filled with mountain streams and breathtaking lakes, including Oregon's gemlike Crater Lake—the nation's deepest—which fills the basin of a collapsed volcano. The Columbia River drains an area of 259,000 square miles from its source in the Canadian Rockies to the Columbia River Bar, west of Portland, where it surges into the Pacific. The Northeast has the broad Hudson River, the quiet Concord, the winding Allegheny, the Connecticut and hundreds of others. Its coastal plains and low mountains contain innumerable streams and lakes.

Lake Okeechobee, in the Florida Everglades, covers some 730 square miles, with an average depth of only seven feet. Its Seminole Indian name means 'very big water.' The Everglades are home to alligators, blue herons, snowy egrets, frogs and toads, and apple snails the size of golf balls. The Shark River is a major source of the slow-moving water that streams through Everglades National Park.

Lake Superior, northernmost of the five Great Lakes, is the largest body of fresh water in the world. It lies across the international border between the United States and Canada and forms part of the great interior waterway system that extends from the Atlantic Ocean through the St Lawrence Seaway, the Great Lakes, and the Mississippi River to the Gulf of Mexico.

Lake Tahoe, an oval-shaped glacial lake, lies in a valley of the Sierra Nevada on the California-Nevada border. It is 23 miles long and 12 miles wide. Its boulder-strewn shoreline is rimmed with vacation homes, camps and resorts.

Alaska's waterways include some three million freshwater lakes, many of which have never been explored because of the difficulty of roadbuilding in America's largest state. Many of Alaska's lakes and rivers are frozen for much of the year. The Hawaiian Islands present a total contrast, with steep waterfalls plunging from volcanic heights and tropical pools that shelter water lilies and feathery umbrella plants. Whatever their form, the lakes and rivers of the United States comprise one of the nation's most valuable resources. They have provided both sustenance and enjoyment since man first appeared on the land.

111 The reedy Blitzen River in Oregon's Malheur National Wildlife Refuge is a port of call for migratory waterfowl on the Pacific flyway.

112/113 The Old North Bridge in Concord, Massachusetts, looking toward the Revolutionary War memorial, 'The Minuteman' by Daniel Chester French.

114 A secluded wedding chapel in a streamside setting in Dodgeville, Wisconsin.

115 Starrs Mill, in Senoia, Georgia, is reflected in its quiet millpond.

116/117 Fishing from massive shoreline boulders deposited by the glaciers around Nevada's Lake Tahoe.

118 An Arizona autumn strikes a harmonious color note at Red Rock Crossing, below Cathedral Rock.

119 Sunset over Arizona's White Horse Lake.

120/121 Wizard Island, in Oregon's incomparable Crater Lake, formed in the basin of an extinct volcano.

122/123 Lake Superior, Michigan, overlooked by the Eagle Harbor Lighthouse, built in 1871 to guide shipping on the northernmost Great Lake.

124 Sculptured Mount Shuksan, Cascade Range, from Highwood Lake in Washington State.

125 Pacific salmon leave the sea for the arduous journey upstream to their freshwater spawning grounds in the Pacific Northwest.

126/127 One of America's historic inland waterways, the Chesapeake and Ohio Canal, seen here at a restored lift lock fronting the Great Falls Tavern and Museum in Maryland.

128 Dramatic Rainbow Falls, in Hilo's Wailuku River Park, Hawaii.

129 Yosemite Falls, the highest waterfall in North America, plummets more than 1750 feet into California's Yosemite Valley.

130 An icy river winds through the forests of the Brooks Range in Arctic Alaska.

131 Vermont's West Riiver at twilight in Londonderry.

132/133 The Santa Elena Canyon of the Rio Grande, at the border between Texas and Mexico.

MOUNTAINS

The high places of the world have exerted their fascination upon man since primitive people saw them as the dwelling places of the gods. Their inaccessible heights have influenced the course of history in many ways, driving whole nations to find new ways over and around them for purposes of exploration, settlement and warfare.

The two great mountain systems of the United States, the Appalachians and the Rockies, formed barriers to westward movement until enterprising frontiersmen and explorers proved that they were not impassable. The highest peak in the Appalachians is North Carolina's Mount Mitchell, at 6,684 feet—relatively low by the standard of peaks farther west, but quite high enough to challenge the pioneers of Daniel Boone's day. The Appalachians include the Allegheny and Blue Ridge Ranges, which extend from Pennsylvania into Virginia, and the haunting Great Smoky Mountains of Tennessee and North Carolina. New England's major peaks are Mount Washington, in the White Mountains of New Hampshire, and Vermont's Mount Mansfield.

As one moves farther west, the mountains become both higher and steeper. Fourteen-thousand-foot Pikes Peak, in the Colorado Rockies, was a famous landmark for settlers heading west under the banner 'Pike's Peak or Bust!' Idaho's Borah Peak, in the snow-capped Lost River Range, was another milestone on the covered-wagon trail.

Naturalist John Muir said of the soaring Rockies, 'Climb the mountains and get their good tidings. Nature's peace will flow into you as sunshine flows into trees.' Nature's peace is seen most clearly during the summer months, when bright wildflowers carpet all but the highest granite summits, while the green timberline marks its slow but steady advance to elevations of more than 11,000 feet. During the winter, though, freezing winds of 200 miles per hour may scream through towers of rock and bend the limber pines into tortured shapes.

Beyond the Rockies, the 700-mile-long Cascade Range descends from southern British Columbia into northern California. Volcanic in origin, these peaks include majestic Mount Rainier in Washington State—the highest, at 14,400 feet—Oregon's graceful Mount Hood, the Three Sisters, Mount Shasta, and the nation's only active volcanoes outside Alaska and Hawaii: Mount Saint Helens, Washington, and Lassen Peak, California. The lower slopes of the Cascades are covered by thick forests of Douglas fir, western hemlock, red cedar and other beautiful trees.

Unlike the Rockies and the Cascades, the Sierra Nevada is not a chain of distinct mountains but a single block of solid granite. It stretches for almost 400 miles near California's eastern border, ranging in width from 50 to 80 miles. Here a massive piece of the earth's crust thrust upward and tilted toward the East like a great blue-grey wave. The snow-capped Sierra rises to heights of more than 14,000 feet.

The massive Alaska Range has hundreds of mountains, the tallest of which is Mount McKinley, the highest peak in North America at 20,320 feet. Mount McKinley is the focal point of Denali National Park in south-central Alaska, which has an area of almost a million acres. Closer to the coast are other ranges of the vast Pacific Mountain system, including the Saint Elias, Chugach, and Kenai.

All of the Hawaiian islands are volcanic in origin, formed deep within the Pacific and rising beneath the waves to their present heights of up to 13,000 feet above sea level. Two of Hawaii's volcanoes are still active: Mauna Kea has long been dormant, but Mauna Loa has erupted twice in the past 37 years, and its Kilauea crater, on the southeast slope, has spewed rivers of molten lava and clouds of hot ash with great frequency. From Hawaii to New England, the rich diversity of America's mountains underscores their varied origins as a testament to the geologic forces that shaped the face of a great country.

135 A hot air balloon drifts over the rugged Chugach Mountains of southern Alaska.

136/137 One of the most beautiful peaks of the Cascade Range, Mount Hood, in Oregon, cloaked in freshly fallen snow.

138 Davis Mountains State Park, near Alpine, Texas, at sunset.

139 Agile mountain goats thrive on the rocky heights of Mount Olympus, in Washington's Olympic Peninsula.

140 Wyoming's jagged Grand Tetons against a field of mountain dandelions in Grand Teton National Park.

141 Cattle graze in the foothills of the Sangre de Cristo Mountains, a range of the Rockies extending from Colorado into New Mexico.

142/143 Dall sheep on an Alaska mountainside. More than 30 different animal species range through the Pacific mountain system.

144 The idyllic Blue Ridge Mountains and Shenandoah Valley of Virginia.

145 The Great Smoky Mountains of North Carolina and Tennessee take their name from the haze that surrounds them all summer as vapor rises from their thick forests.

146/147 A walking path along the ridge of Franconia Notch, in New Hampshire's White Mountains.

148 top Awe-inspiring Dante's View, in the desolate Black Mountains of California.

148 bottom Morning light bathes the ridges and valley of Hawaii's Ko'olau Range, viewed from Nu'uanu Pali State Park.

149 An old Colorado town maintains a foothold in the Rocky Mountains.

150/151 Rain clouds linger over an Idaho ranch in the Upper Coeur d'Alene Valley.

152/153 Evergreens etched in frost on the slopes of Mount Mansfield, Vermont.

154 The sedimentary rock of Montana's splendid Glacier National Park is the oldest on earth.

155 Yellow cinquefoil blooms in a flat valley, called a hole, below the 7000-foot wall of Wyoming's Grand Tetons.

156/157   Mount Saint Helens, Washington, after
the devastating eruption of 1980, which proved
that the volcanic Cascade Range was not entirely
dormant.

158/159   Snow-capped peaks north of Fairbanks,
Alaska, form a lunar landscape.

DESERTS AND CANYONS

The American West is the scene of thousands of square miles of desert, which may appear almost lifeless to the undiscerning eye, but is, in fact, teeming with plants and animals that have adapted themselves to the imperatives of their arid environment. Spotted cactus wrens and mottled rock wrens frequent the magenta-flowered chollas and clumps of prickly pear, with their pink, orange, and yellow blossoms. White yucca moths pollinate the cream-colored yucca flowers on their tall, leafy stems—plants that provided the desert-dwelling Indians of the Southwest with food, drink, fiber and even soap. Similarly valuable was the agave, also known as the century plant or mescal. Its sharp spines were used for needles and awls, its fermented juice produced a strong liquor, and most parts of the plant were roasted and stored for food. It was this plant that gave the Mescalero Apaches their name.

Many of the desert animals carry out their activities under cover of darkness, or beneath the rippling sand dunes. Kangaroo rats emerge from their burrows at dusk in search of yucca seeds. Pocket mice, toads and sidewinders, hares and rabbits all leave their elusive imprints in the sand. The wail of a hunting coyote is one of the few sounds to break the silence of a desert night.

The great American deserts include White Sands National Monument in southern New Mexico, Arizona's Painted Desert, along the Little Colorado River, and California's Mojave Desert, north of Baja, which once lay beneath the Pacific Ocean. In Monument Valley, the Navajo Indians maintain their traditional way of life as shepherds and weavers, making handicrafts of great beauty and utility. Their predecessors include the Anasazi, or Ancient Ones, who built cliff dwellings in what is now northern Arizona, New Mexico, Utah and Colorado; the Hohokam, who were the first to irrigate the southwestern desert and make it productive; and the Mogollon, who were hunters and farmers.

Uplift and erosion were the principal architects of the West's multicolored canyons, soaring arches and pinnacles of stone. The eerily beautiful pink sandstone formations of Bryce Canyon, Utah, are some 60 million years old. Nearby Zion Canyon exposes still older rocks in majestic cliffs that rise more than 3000 feet from their base. This part of the West was once the floor of an inland sea. Then massive pressure from within the earth thrust up a huge tablelike mesa along deep faults at what is now Bryce Canyon. Over the centuries, rain, wind and frost ate away at the edges of this formation to produce the strange spires and standing stones that we see today.

The Grand Canyon started out as a plain through which a quiet river cut a shallow bed. As subterranean forces lifted the plain in a cataclysmic upheaval, the river ran faster and cut deeper. Ages later, the Colorado River flowed through a chasm some 200 miles long, averaging nine miles wide and more than a mile deep. The depth of the canyon affects temperature and precipitation to such a degree that the life forms occurring down its walls at various points represent the entire range of the North American continent.

At Arches National Park, Utah, rocky canopies and slender stone bridges leap across deep canyons scoured out along faults in solid sandstone by wind and water. Vertical walls or fins that remained between these crevasses were weathered to small openings that enlarged over the years into delicate arcades. Graceful Landscape Arch is a ribbon of sandstone almost 300 feet across.

Wherever one looks in the West, he is inspired by a sense of wonder that transcends anything we know about the geological forces that shaped this land and are still reshaping it to the present day.

161 Ever-changing Kelso Dunes, in the Mojave Desert of California.

162-164 Morning sun breaks through storm clouds at Dead Horse Point State Park in Utah.

165   Pinnacles of fantastically eroded limestone
guard the mazelike ravines of Utah's Bryce
Canyon.

166 Arid Death Valley, California, was a huge lake in glacial times. Now scarce rainfall is sucked up in a moment by the thirsty earth.

167 A red-spined barrel cactus and tall, stately Saguaro grow in the Tonto National Forest near Payson, Arizona.

168/169 Death Valley's shifting dunes and merciless heat were dreaded by the pioneers who gave the desert its name.

170/171 The stark Saguaro cactus is an emblem of the American West. These plants may grow to a height of 50 feet and live for some 200 years.

172 Bandelier National Momument, near Santa Fe, contains relics of prehistoric life in New Mexico.

173 The Indians of Taos Pueblo, New Mexico, have occupied this site for 700 years.

174/175 A panoramic view of the great Cliff Palace in Mesa Verde National Park, Colorado.

176/177 The eerie blue-white landscape of New Mexico's White Sands National Monument, the world's largest deposit of gypsum.

178 The multicolored pinnacles below Point Supreme in Utah's Cedar Breaks National Monument.

179 The dizzying height of the North Rim of the Grand Canyon, reached by the Spanish explorer Cardenas in 1540.

180/181 Delicate Arch commands an imposing view of Utah's Arches National Park, which one explorer described as 'the work of giant hands.'

182/183 Blue Mesa, in Arizona's Petrified Forest National Park, which contains an incredible variety of ancient trees that have been turned to stone by the elements.

PEOPLE

Glimpses of the American people in all their diversity could fill an entire volume of this size. They would reflect an enormous range of ethnic and cultural backgrounds, from the far distant past to the headlines of this morning's newspaper. The kaleidoscope that could capture America's people would reflect the history of immigrants from every country of the world; the black experience; the Polynesian search for a new homeland in the Pacific; the past and present ways of life of the native Americans; and much more.

If one starts his Journey 'Down East' in Maine, he will see the weathered faces of fishermen who set their lobster pots in the cold waters of this coast. Throughout rural New England, he will find people with a strong sense of regional identity—farmers, factory workers, small-town merchants descended from the original Yankee peddlers of Connecticut. New Englanders tend to stay put more than other Americans; in some communities you're still considered a newcomer after 25 or 30 years. The original British colonial stock in this part of the world was enriched by the successive waves of immigration that brought textile, leather and metal workers from Europe and Canada.

In Appalachia, sturdy mountain people still work the land, mines and timber of a rugged region that demands resourcefulness and energy from its inhabitants. Florida has a mixture of long-time residents in the citrus, cattle and fishing industries and suntanned tourists who come and go on the palm-fringed beaches like the daily tides.

In the rural Midwest and the Great Plains states, farmers are holding on to their land and way of life despite the adversities of recent years, and the tradition of helping out a neighbor in need remains strong. Cooperative use of storage facilities, expensive machinery, and transportation equipment has helped the American farmer remain productive.

The Indian and Hispanic heritage of the Southwest is visible in the bronze faces of Pueblo elders in Taos, New Mexico, and the hard-driving cattlemen and ranchers of Arizona and Texas. Life in the arid Southwest has never been easy, but it seems to suit those who live here: few of them would trade it for anywhere else.

The people of the West Coast tend to be adventurous and easy-going, attuned to the outdoors and the many recreational opportunities of their scenic land. Of course, California is not populated entirely by blond surfers, any more than Hawaii is populated entirely by hula dancers, as popular stereotypes would have it. The industrious farmers and ranchers of the Imperial Valley have their counterparts on the lush pineapple and taro plantations of the islands.

In the Pacific Northwest, Indians of the original coastal tribes are experiencing a cultural renaissance, remastering their traditional crafts of woodcarving and painting to produce stark and powerful totem poles and swift dugouts hewn from a single massive tree trunk. In Alaska, the land claims of native people, including the Indians, Eskimos and Aleuts, have been addressed by the Native Lands Claim Settlement Act, which allocated $900 million and 44 million acres in compensation for a history of exploitation that began with the Russian fur traders of the eighteenth and nineteenth centuries.

A growing sense of mutual support and responsibility seems to be evolving everywhere in America, as former rigid boundaries of race, caste and class give way to a more mature view: that the things which unite us are far more important and powerful than the superficial distinctions that have kept us apart in the past.

185 *A southwestern farmer brings his pungent chilies to market.*

186 *A grizzled tour guide in the Florida Everglades.*

187 *Summer's child.*

188 top   Carrying on the family trade in leather goods in Talkeetna, Alaska.

188 bottom Children from the Honolulu Community Center form a cultural mosaic that includes Chinese, Japanese, Hawaiian, Caucasian and Filipino ethnic groups.

189 top   A Maine family in nautical headgear watches a parade without worrying about the rain.

189 bottom   A Kotzebue Indian family of coastal Alaska prepares to celebrate a holiday.

190 Independence Day inspires a display of patriotism by Tennessee veterans.

191 Arkansas' Ozark Folk Center celebrates the country music heritage of America's mountain people.

192/193 A skilled New England boatmaker practices his time-honored craft.

194　A delighted tourist shows her approval of a day in Key West.

195　A Chinese Hawaiian smiles a greeting from the shade of her parasol.

196　A resident of New Mexico's Taos Pueblo, which was standing when the Spanish explorers arrived.

197　Gathering vanda orchids for Hawaii's flourishing trade in exotic plants.

198　A festival blanket toss at Barrow, Alaska, on the Arctic Ocean. The blanket toss was once used by Eskimo hunters as a way of spotting game.

199　Kite Day in breezy Anchorage fills the sky with shapes and colors.

WILDERNESS

America's countryside includes millions of acres of land that is virtually uninhabited, some of it largely unexplored. Such wilderness areas range from the cliffs and coves encircling the woodlands of Acadia National Park in Maine to the massive monoliths of Utah's Zion National Park. On Isle Royale, in Michigan's Lake Superior, the wolf is making a successful comeback from generations of depredation by bounty hunters, farmers and ranchers. On the Channel Islands, off the coast of California, seabirds and seals find a congenial habitat on the tips of underwater mountains.

The Rocky Mountains remain largely untamed, despite the limited inroads of miners, settlers and city-builders over the last few hundred years. In Big Bend National Park, Texas, an astonishing variety of wildlife thrives where rivers, mountains and desert converge. Utah's Capitol Reef remains, as it was to the Navajo, 'the Land of the Sleeping Rainbow.'

Many lakes and mountain streams in the scenic Cascades are virtually untouched by man, and the Mojave Desert belongs mainly to the plants and animals that have adapted to survival on its arid heights. The famous Hot Springs of Arkansas flow through the Zig Zag Mountains, where rabbits, raccoons and opossums make their homes in the forest, along with deer and foxes.

On distant Hawaii, which Mark Twain called 'the loveliest fleet of islands that lies anchored in any ocean,' the national parks of Haleakala and Hawaii Volcanoes protect a world of jungle birds and tropical blossoms laced by waterfalls and studded with twisted koa trees up to 100 feet tall. But the nation's greatest wilderness acreage is found, of course, in Alaska: 586,400 square miles, more than twice as large as Texas.

The huge peninsula that forms most of Alaska remains largely wilderness, with only one-fifth of the state accessible by road. The dominant features are the Pacific and Arctic mountain systems, a central plateau, and the Arctic slope. The total population of the state is well under a million.

Alaska has no fewer than eight national parks, the oldest of which is Denali, 'the Great One,' as native Alaskans called Mount McKinley. The north face of this awesome peak soars some 18,000 feet above the wide tundra plain below it. There are no trees on the slopes of the Alaska Range, which are perpetually clothed in ice and snow. Vast, slow glaciers flow down their sides, gouging out deep gorges and filling them with ice. Meltwater from the north face glaciers feeds countless streams and rivers in the tundra below. Grizzly bears browse on the native blueberries, and caribou roam the flat plains.

Alaska's jagged coastline is longer than those of all the lower 48 states combined. One can travel back into the Ice Age along the Inside Passage, where the towering glaciers of Glacier Bay National Park are easily approached by boat. Sitka spruces in a nearby rain forest are surrounded by moss and festooned with dangling tree mosses. Gates of the Arctic National Park, north of the Arctic Circle, straddles the Brooks Range, the northernmost extension of the Rockies. These and other sanctuaries guarantee the preservation of the American wilderness and that sense of wonder which inspired Thoreau when he wrote 'In wildness is the preservation of the world.'

201 Sunrise at rugged Chiricahua National Monument, named for one of Arizona's Apache peoples.

202/203 A field of summer wildflowers below the distant cloud-covered peaks of the San Francisco Mountains in Arizona.

204 A weathered relic of boom times in the ghost town of Bowie, California.

205 An old ranch below The Raggeds in Colorado's Muddy Creek Canyon.

206/207 Daffodils spring from a forest floor in East Hampton, Connecticut. Remnants of a stone wall indicate that this was once farmland.

208 top   Petrified wood dots the dry landscape of northeastern Arizona.

208 bottom   The Mojave Desert covers high ground from the Colorado River in Nevada to southern California's Sierra Nevada.

209 top   Deep snow blankets isolated Mount Baker in the Northern Cascades.

209 bottom   Yosemite Valley's El Capitan, 3600 feet high, is the world's largest solid granite rock.

210   A weathered cabin withstands the elements in Alaska's Arctic Village.

211   Mountains recede into the mist in Gates of the Arctic National Park, Alaska.

212/213   Mount McKinley, North America's highest peak, towers over the Alaska Range near Wonder Lake.

214/215   A tropical storm gathers over Everglades National Park, which covers 1,400,000 acres in southern Florida.

216/217   Hikers in Alaska's Kantishna Hills survey the immensity of Denali National Park.

SEASONS

Seasonal changes in America's countryside are most apparent where there are deciduous trees that flame into brilliant color before they drop their leaves for the quiescent winter, and where there is a marked difference between summer and winter temperatures. In New England, where cold weather comes early, multicolored fall foliage attracts many visitors during the fine Indian summer days. For some, it will be the last expedition until the short, dark days of winter give way to the chilly breezes of early spring.

The winter landscape has its own kind of beauty, tracing the leafless limbs of trees against a cold blue sky, frosting the evergreens with symmetrical rings of snow, and blanketing the countryside in drifts that hinder travel but make a fireside doubly welcome. Those birds that have not flown south are hard pressed to find food, and squirrels dig up the acorns that they have prudently stored for lean times. Hungry deer may leave the woods and venture close to houses and farms in their quest for forage.

Snow may be welcome for Christmas, but by February it has lost much of its charm: there is wide speculation about whether or not the ground hog will see his shadow when he comes up from his burrow to forecast the end of winter. But even the dull days of February will end in a thaw and the freshening winds of March. The first crocuses and snowdrops push up boldly through the melting snow and signal the flamboyant color displays of April.

Daffodils and dogwood are among the best-loved harbingers of spring, along with the iridescent tulips, the pink and white azaleas, and the fragrant lavender hyacinths. The greening of the countryside is so gradual that it can take one by surprise: a week's absence, however, will mark the difference clearly. The tips of willows show first a mist and then a green garment of spring. Meadows and lawns proceed quickly from the first tentative shoots of new grass to a luxuriant carpet that obliterates the yellows and browns of winter. By June, the days will be almost entirely fair, and schoolchildren will be counting down eagerly to the summer vacation.

At last, school is out, and the bright, unhurried days of summer settle over the land. It's a pleasure to sleep late and awaken to the prospect of a picnic, a day at the shore, a walk in the woods. Crowded fall and winter schedules are put away, and people give themselves time simply to be through the long days and warm nights of that season like no other. Only too soon, the Labor Day weekend will announce the return of the workaday world, but until then it is easy to believe in the endlessness of summer.

219 Trees aflame with autumn color stand behind a shack in the White Mountains of New Hampshire.

220/221 Flowering dogwood adds to the spring beauty of the historic Biltmore Estate in Asheville, North Carolina.

222/223 Vibrant corn poppies share a summer meadow with daisies and true chamomile in the Pacific Northwest.

224 Moonrise over a wintry landscape in Goshen, Vermont.

225 top A summer lightning storm strikes over Arizona.

225 bottom Sunset promises relief from the somnolent heat of the Louisiana bayou country.

226/227 Wildflowers strike a colorful note at the Spocott Windmill near Cambridge, Maryland.

228 Red maples and balsam firs line the Swift River in New Hampshire with brilliant fall colors.

229 Slender birches frame a distant view of Mount Washington from Conway, New Hampshire.

230/231   The pumpkin harvest is gathered on a
Rhode Island farm in time for Halloween.

232   October on a Great Plains farm in Judith
Basin County, Montana.

233 Wardsboro, Vermont, prepares to dig itself out from under a heavy snowfall.

234/235 A dusting of snow softens the bristly forms of southwestern cacti.

236/237 Winter mantles the rugged Wilson Mountains in the Colorado Rockies.